J-B GAL
Whiting, Jim
Galileo
2007

A Robbie Reader

What's So Great About . . . ?

GALILEO

Jim Whiting

P.O. Box 196
Hockessin, Delaware 19707
Visit us on the web: www.mitchelllane.com
Comments? email us: mitchelllane@mitchelllane.com

Copyright © 2008 by Mitchell Lane Publishers. All rights reserved. No part of this book may be reproduced without written permission from the publisher. Printed and bound in the United States of America.

Printing 1 2 3 4 5 6 7 8 9

A Robbie Reader/What's So Great About . . . ?

Amelia Earhart	Anne Frank	Annie Oakley
Christopher Columbus	Daniel Boone	Davy Crockett
Elizabeth Blackwell	Ferdinand Magellan	Francis Scott Key
Galileo	George Washington Carver	Harriet Tubman
Helen Keller	Henry Hudson	Jacques Cartier
Johnny Appleseed	Paul Bunyan	Robert Fulton
Rosa Parks	Sam Houston	

Library of Congress Cataloging-in-Publication Data
Whiting, Jim, 1943-
  Galileo / by Jim Whiting.
    p. cm. — (A Robbie Reader. What's so great about—?)
Includes bibliographical references and index.
ISBN 978-1-58415-575-1 (library bound)
 1. Galilei, Galileo, 1564-1642—Juvenile literature. 2. Astronomy—History—Juvenile literature. 3. Astronomers—Italy—Biography—Juvenile literature. I. Title.
QB36.G2W485 2008
520.92—dc22
[B]
                                                                                2007000814

ABOUT THE AUTHOR: Jim Whiting has been a remarkably versatile and accomplished journalist, writer, editor, and photographer for more than 30 years. A voracious reader since early childhood, Mr. Whiting has written and edited more than 250 nonfiction children's books on a wide range of topics. He lives in Washington state with his wife and two teenage sons.

PHOTO CREDITS: Cover, p. 4—Barbara Marvis; p. 8—Jonathan Scott; p. 25—Ricardo André Frantz; pp. 26, 27—NASA

PUBLISHER'S NOTE: The following story has been thoroughly researched and to the best of our knowledge represents a true story. While every possible effort has been made to ensure accuracy, the publisher will not assume liability for damages caused by inaccuracies in the data, and makes no warranty on the accuracy of the information contained herein.

                                                                                        PPC

TABLE OF CONTENTS

Chapter One
Facing a Fiery Fate 5

Chapter Two
Math and Making Things 9

Chapter Three
Observing the Heavens 13

Chapter Four
On Dangerous Ground 19

Chapter Five
A Hard Decision 23

Chronology 28
Timeline in History 29
Find Out More 30
    Books 30
    Works Consulted 30
    On the Internet 30
Glossary 31
Index 32

Words in **bold** type can be found in the glossary.

Galileo sits alone during his trial in 1633. He was accused of holding beliefs that were not the same as those of the Catholic Church. It was a very serious charge. Many people were found guilty and executed for such beliefs.

CHAPTER ONE

Facing a Fiery Fate

Galileo Galilei (gal-uh-LAY-oh gal-uh-LAY) was nervous. He was on trial for heresy (HAIR-uh-see)—or disagreeing with the beliefs of the Catholic Church. In Galileo's time, the Church looked for and punished people who disagreed with its teachings.

Galileo was a famous scientist and inventor. People all over Europe were watching the trial closely.

The court was in Rome, Italy. It was called the **Inquisition** (in-kwih-ZIH-shun). Two hundred years earlier, the Inquisition had found Joan of Arc guilty of heresy. She was burned at the stake. Thousands of other **heretics** (HAIR-uh-tiks) were also **executed** (EK-seh-kyoo-ted).

5

CHAPTER ONE

Robert Bellarmine, a cardinal in the Catholic Church, had warned Galileo in 1616 that his theories needed to agree with the teachings of the Church. Bellarmine was later made a saint.

If the Church found him guilty, Galileo would be sentenced to die.

Galileo believed Earth and other planets revolve around the sun. He **published** his **theory** (THEE-uh-ree). Although people today believe this is true, in Galileo's time people thought otherwise.

FACING A FIERY FATE

In the 1600s, people still believed the teachings of a famous Greek **philosopher** (fih-LAH-suh-fur) named Aristotle (AIR-uh-stah-tul). Aristotle lived in the fourth century BCE. Some of his beliefs were correct. For example, he said that Earth is round.

On the other hand, he said that the sun and the planets revolve around Earth. This was called the **geocentric** (jee-oh-SEN-trik)—or Earth-centered—system. The Church believed in this system as well.

When Galileo published his theory, the Church called him a heretic and put him on trial.

The trial went on for weeks. The **prosecutor** (PRAH-seh-kyoo-tur) kept asking tough questions. Galileo tried to defend himself. Finally, near the end of the trial, Galileo faced the prosecutor. Grim-faced church officials looked on. They knew the next few minutes would determine whether Galileo lived or died.

Galileo was born in Pisa, Italy. He spent many years teaching in Padua. He moved to Florence in 1610 and lived there for most of the rest of his life. His trial for heresy was held in Rome.

CHAPTER TWO

Math and Making Things

Galileo was born on February 15, 1564, in Pisa, Italy. He was the oldest of six children. His father, Vincenzo Galilei, was a famous musician. Galileo's mother was named Giulia.

Vincenzo knew that his son was very smart. He taught the boy himself until he was eleven. Then Galileo went to school. Vincenzo wanted him to become a doctor, so in 1581, Galileo began studying medicine at the University of Pisa. He soon realized that he was much more interested in mathematics. He also liked to figure out how things worked.

He left the university in 1585 to study science. He conducted many experiments,

CHAPTER TWO

which was unusual. No scientist—not even Aristotle—had done that before. Aristotle used **logic** (LAH-jik) to test his ideas. He never tested them in real life.

Some of Galileo's findings were surprising. For example, Aristotle thought about what would happen if you dropped two objects of a similar shape from the same height. He thought the heavier one would fall faster. Galileo did experiments and found that Aristotle was wrong. Objects of different weights fell at the same rate.

Galileo also invented many useful things. These included a water pump, a way of balancing objects, and a thermometer. He figured out how a **pendulum** (PEN-juh-lum) clock would work. He made tools that helped sailors find their way at sea. He built a device that helped them row faster.

Galileo had an active personal life. He met a woman named Marina Camba in 1599. The couple had three children: Vincenzo, Arcangela, and Maria Celeste. In later life, he became especially close to Maria Celeste.

MATH AND MAKING THINGS

Galileo invented the sector, a device used to figure out how to aim cannons. Hanging from the sector is a six-ounce lodestone, or magnet, which is holding up a fifteen-pound metal box. Galileo was one of the first scientists to study magnetism.

She helped her father by copying his writings. However, she pledged her life to the Catholic Church and became a nun. She and her father wrote many letters that were later published.

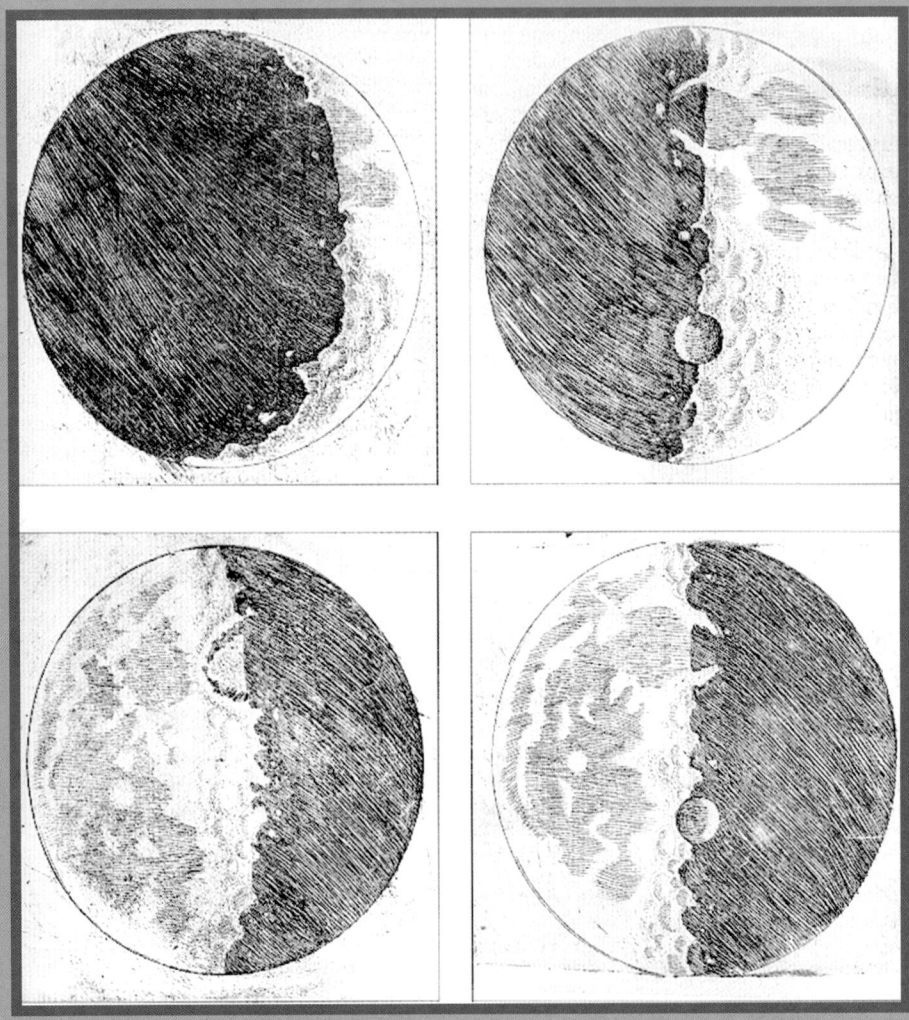
Until Galileo looked at the moon through a telescope, people believed that the moon was smooth. Galileo found that it had mountains, valleys, and broad plains. He drew pictures of what he had seen and published them in 1610 in his book *Sidereus Nuncius*.

CHAPTER THREE

Observing the Heavens

Galileo's ability to make things came in handy in 1609. He heard about a new invention from Holland called the telescope. The telescope made it possible to see things that were very far away. He quickly made several models. Each one was better than the last. His telescopes were powerful enough to look into outer space.

He spent many nights looking at the moon, the planets, and the stars. Right away he discovered fascinating things. People—including Aristotle—thought the moon's surface was smooth. It wasn't. Galileo saw high mountains and deep craters. He realized that the Milky Way had millions of stars. He thought

CHAPTER THREE

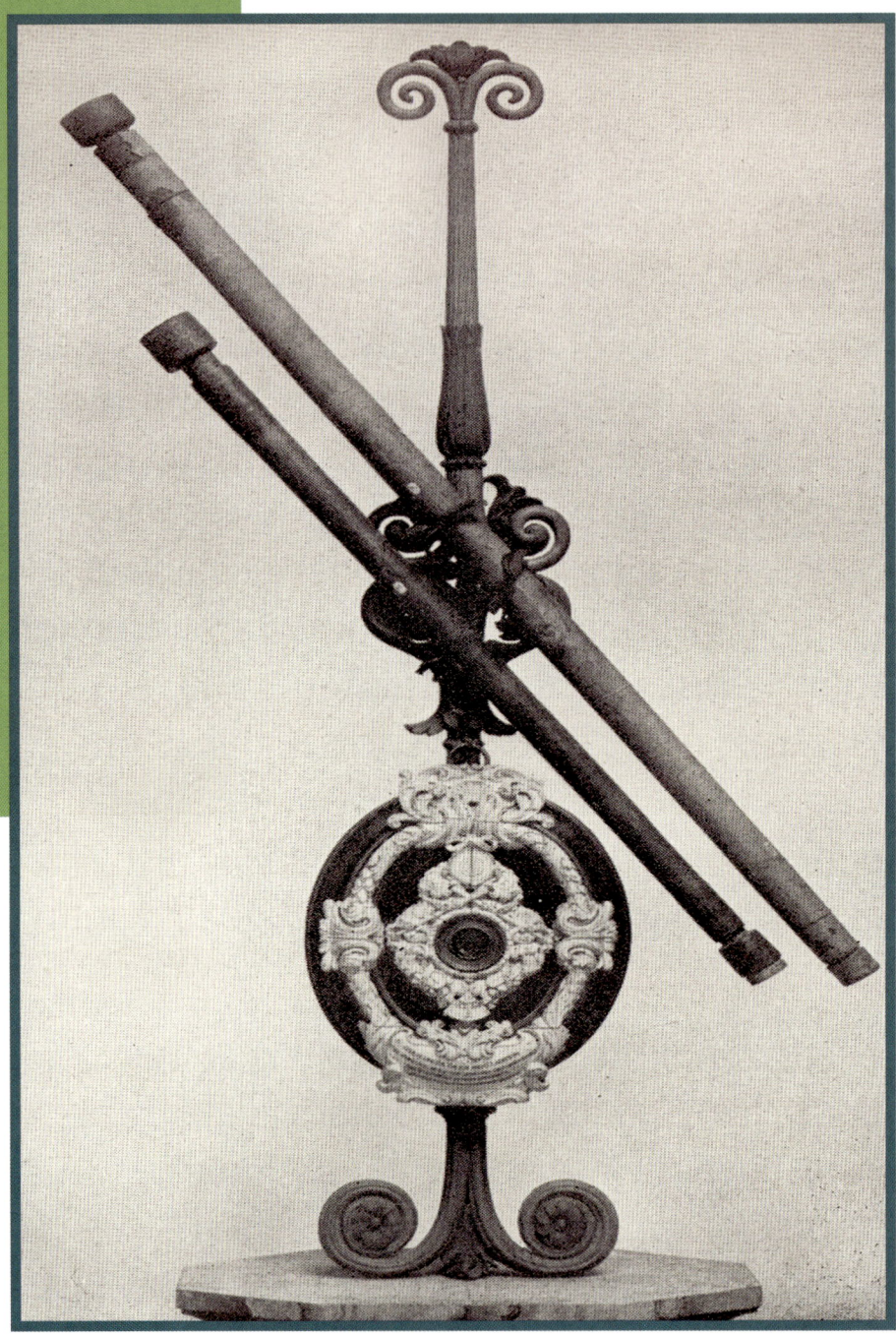

Galileo made several improved versions of the telescope, which had been invented in Holland in 1608. He used them to scan the heavens.

OBSERVING THE HEAVENS

Galileo observed the Milky Way Galaxy. A galaxy is a group of millions of stars. The sun and Earth are part of the Milky Way.

that the planet Saturn was oblong, but in this he was wrong. Later **astronomers** (uh-STRAH-nuh-murs) with more powerful telescopes discovered the oval shape was caused by the rings around the planet.

15

CHAPTER THREE

A diagram of the solar system showing how the planets orbit the sun. Galileo probably observed Uranus and Neptune, but didn't realize that they were planets.

OBSERVING THE HEAVENS

He published some of his findings in 1610. The book was called the *Starry Messenger*. It gave little hint of the storm that was about to come.

Planet Saturn

Several years earlier, in 1597, Galileo had read a book by Nicolaus Copernicus (NIH-koh-lous kuh-PUR-nih-kus). Copernicus said that Earth and the planets orbit the sun. This is called the **heliocentric** (HEE-lee-oh-sen-trik)—or sun-centered—system. Copernicus published his ideas in 1543. The Church strongly disapproved of Copernicus's book. Before the Inquisition could try him for heresy, he died.

The Church did make one thing clear. It would be dangerous for anyone to publicly support Copernicus's theory. Very dangerous.

Galileo made drawings of sunspots, which are dark patches on the sun. He observed that they seemed to move. This apparent movement was a clue that Earth revolved around the sun.

CHAPTER FOUR

On Dangerous Ground

Galileo's stargazing convinced him that Copernicus was right. One clue was sunspots—dark blotches that appear to be on the surface of the sun. Each day they seemed to move a little bit. He figured that the sunspots themselves weren't moving. They just looked like they were because Earth was moving. The same thing happened when he watched several moons moving around the planet Jupiter. The way they appeared to move also convinced Galileo that Earth was not standing still.

In 1613, he published another book, called *Letters on Sunspots*. The book openly supported Copernicus. Galileo knew it might cause trouble, so he went to Rome to talk with

CHAPTER FOUR

Nicolaus Copernicus was born in Poland in 1473. He developed his theory that Earth revolves around the sun in the early 1500s, but he waited many years to publish it.

ON DANGEROUS GROUND

Pope Paul V. He asked the pope to support him. All he was doing, he said, was trying to arrive at the truth.

His meeting didn't help. In 1616, the Inquisition gave him a severe warning. The court told him not to support Copernicus's system.

Galileo seemed to obey the order. He put most of his energy into studying other things.

In 1623, a friend of Galileo's was elected as the new pope, Urban VIII. Soon he asked Galileo to write a book. It would compare the geocentric and heliocentric systems. The Pope said he wanted the book to be balanced, but he really didn't. He wanted Galileo to show that Copernicus's theory was wrong.

Galileo began writing the book, which he named *Dialogue* [DY-uh-log] *Concerning the Two Chief World Systems*. The book was published in 1632. As Urban had requested, it was one-sided—but it wasn't the side he wanted. It favored the theories of Copernicus.

A portrait of Galileo drawn by artist Ottavio Leoni in 1624. That year Galileo met six times with Pope Urban VIII and explained some of his theories. The pope gave him permission to write a book but warned him to be careful about what he said.

CHAPTER FIVE

A Hard Decision

The pope was furious. In 1633, he ordered Galileo to appear before the Inquisition. By then Galileo was sixty-nine. He was in ill health. That didn't matter to the Church. It couldn't let him get away with writing the *Dialogue*.

Unlike most heretics, Galileo had an advantage. He knew many important church officials. They really didn't want to execute him. Behind the scenes, they tried to work out a deal. Galileo expected a light penalty. He believed nothing really horrible would happen to him.

He was wrong. The Inquisition said he could live—but only on one condition. Galileo would have to take back what he had said. It would ruin his reputation (reh-pyoo-TAY-shun).

CHAPTER FIVE

Galileo chose to remain alive. He said he had been wrong. "My error, then, has been—and I confess it, one of **vainglorious** [vayn-GLOOR-ee-us] ambition and pure ignorance," he told the Inquisition.

His confession wasn't enough. He was sentenced to life in prison. Soon the pope gave him a little bit of a break. He said that Galileo would be under house arrest. He could live at home rather than in jail, but his movements would be limited. Living like this wouldn't be very enjoyable.

Galileo went blind in 1637. His health continued to get worse. He died on January 8, 1642.

Today we know that Galileo was right: Earth does revolve around the sun. Other planets also orbit the sun. In 1992, Pope John Paul II officially pardoned the scientist. He said that Galileo had been right all along.

Scientists and many other people honor Galileo. They say he was the first person to use actual experiments to find out scientific truths. Modern scientists continue to use his methods.

A HARD DECISION

Galileo's tomb in Santa Croce, Florence, Italy. Galileo died in 1642. He was first buried in a chapel that belonged to the Medicis, one of Florence's most famous families. His remains were moved to the Church of Santa Croce in 1737.

CHAPTER FIVE

The *Galileo* spacecraft, launched in 1989 aboard the space shuttle *Atlantis*, studied Jupiter and its moons. It found warm ice, water, and icebergs on the moon Europa before ending its mission in 2003.

A HARD DECISION

The U.S. space program honored one of his many accomplishments in 1989. The *Galileo* spacecraft blasted off to study Jupiter and its moons, which Galileo had discovered nearly four centuries earlier. The spacecraft began orbiting Jupiter in 1995 and sent valuable information back to Earth for eight years.

The space shuttle *Atlantis* blasted off on October 18, 1989, carrying the *Galileo* spacecraft. During its fourteen-year journey, *Galileo* traveled nearly three billion miles.

CHRONOLOGY

1564 Galileo Galilei is born on February 15.

1581 He becomes a student at the University of Pisa.

1592 He becomes a professor at the University of Padua.

1599 He begins a relationship with Marina Gamba; they eventually have three children.

1609 Galileo begins looking at the skies through his telescope.

1610 Galileo moves to Florence, where he lives for most of the rest of his life.

1613 He publishes *Letters on Sunspots*.

1616 The Inquisition warns Galileo about his theories.

1624 Pope Urban VIII asks Galileo to write *Dialogue Concerning the Two Chief World Systems*.

1632 Galileo publishes *Dialogue Concerning the Two Chief World Systems*.

1633 He appears before the Inquisition and is found guilty. He is placed under house arrest for the rest of his life.

1642 Galileo dies on January 8.

TIMELINE IN HISTORY

1543 Astronomer Nicolaus Copernicus publishes *On the Revolutions of the Heavenly Spheres*—a book whose ideas anger the Catholic Church.

1564 William Shakespeare is born in England in April.

1582 Pope Gregory XIII adjusts the calendar so that it more accurately reflects Earth's yearly orbit.

1594 Italian thinker Giordano Bruno is imprisoned by the Catholic Church because he supports Copernicus; he is executed six years later.

1609 Henry Hudson explores New York Harbor and the Hudson River.

1620 Pilgrims land at Plymouth, Massachusetts.

1630 Boston, Massachusetts, is founded.

1651 Italian astronomer Giovanni Riccioli observes the moon and publishes a map of what he sees.

1675 The Royal Observatory is established at Greenwich, England, just outside of London.

1687 Isaac Newton describes the theory of gravity.

1692 Twenty people are executed in Salem, Massachusetts, because they are believed to be witches.

FIND OUT MORE

Books

Boothroyd, Jennifer. *Galileo Galilei: A Life of Curiosity.* Minneapolis: Lerner, 2006.

Brighton, Catherine. *Galileo's Treasure Box.* New York: Walker Books for Young Readers, 2001.

Mason, Paul. *Galileo.* Chicago: Heinemann, 2003.

Sís, Peter. *Starry Messenger.* New York: Farrar, Straus and Giroux, 2000.

Steele, Philip. *Galileo: The Genius Who Faced the Inquisition.* Washington, D.C.: National Geographic, 2005.

Works Consulted

Drake, Stillman. *Galileo at Work: His Scientific Biography.* Mineola, New York: Dover Publications, 1995.

Reston, James. *Galileo: A Life.* New York: HarperCollins, 1994.

Sharratt, Michael. *Galileo: Decisive Innovator.* Cambridge, United Kingdom: Cambridge University Press, 1996.

Sobel, Dava. *Galileo's Daughter.* New York: Walker and Company, 1999.

On the Internet

Galileo Galilei
http://starchild.gsfc.nasa.gov/docs/StarChild/whos_who_level2/galileo.html

Galileo Sees the Light
http://www.thursdaysclassroom.com/03feb00/article1a.html

Galileo: Journey to Jupiter
http://www2.jpl.nasa.gov/galileo/

Thursday's Classroom: Happy Birthday, Galileo!
http://www.thursdaysclassroom.com/index_08feb01.html

GLOSSARY

astronomers (uh-STRAH-nuh-murs)—Scientists who study the stars and planets.

executed (EK-seh-kyoo-ted)—Killed upon the order of a court or another authority.

geocentric (jee-oh-SEN-trik)—Earth-centered.

heliocentric (HEE-lee-oh-sen-trik)—Sun-centered.

heretic (HAIR-uh-tik)—Someone who does not believe in what the Catholic Church teaches.

Inquisition (in-kwih-ZIH-shun)—Special Catholic court set up to try people who do or believe things that are different from what the Church teaches.

logic (LAH-jik)—Straight-line thinking.

pendulum (PEN-juh-lum)—A suspended object that moves back and forth at regular intervals.

philosopher (fih-LAH-suh-fur)—A person who seeks to understand the basic truths about life.

prosecutor (PRAH-seh-kyoo-tur)—A lawyer who tries to convince a judge that a particular person has committed a crime.

published (PUB-lishd)—Prepared written material for sale to many people.

theory (THEE-uh-ree)—A belief based on the study of a number of facts.

vainglorious (vayn-GLOOR-ee-us)—Boastful; having too much pride in one's accomplishments.

INDEX

Aristotle 7, 10, 13
Atlantis (space shuttle) 26, 27
Bellarmine, Robert 6
Camba, Marina 10
Catholic Church 5, 7, 11, 17, 23
Copernicus, Nicolaus 17, 19, 20, 21
Dialogue Concerning the Two Chief World Systems 21, 23
Earth 6, 7, 15, 17, 18, 20, 24
Europa (moon of Jupiter) 26
Florence, Italy 8, 25
Galilei, Arcangela 10
Galilei, Galileo
 and astronomy 12, 13, 15, 16, 17, 18, 19, 27
 birth of 9
 books of 12, 17, 19, 21, 22, 23
 children of 10
 death of 24, 25
 education of 9
 inventions of 10, 11, 13, 14
 marriage of 10
 magnets 11
 theories of 6–7, 10
 trial of 4, 5, 7, 23–24
Galilei, Giulia (mother) 9
Galilei, Maria Celeste 10–11
Galilei, Vincenzo (father) 9
Galilei, Vincenzo (son) 10
Galileo spacecraft 26, 27
geocentric system 7, 21
heliocentric system 17, 21
Inquisition 4, 5, 17, 21, 23–24
John Paul II, Pope 24
Jupiter 19, 26, 27
Letters on Sunspots 19
Leoni, Ottavio 22
Medici family, the 25
Milky Way, the 13, 15
moon (Earth's) 12, 13
Neptune 16
Padua, Italy 8
Paul V, Pope 21
Pisa, Italy 8, 9
Rome, Italy 5, 8, 19
Santa Croce, Church of 25
Saturn 15, 17
Sidereus Nuncius 12
Starry Messenger 17
sun 6, 7, 15, 17, 18, 19, 20, 24
sunspots 18, 19
telescope 12, 13, 14, 15
University of Pisa 9
Uranus 16
Urban VIII, Pope 21, 22, 23, 24